Energy for

Water Power

By Tea Benduhn

Reading consultant: Susan Nations, M.Ed.,
author/literacy coach/consultant in literacy development

Science and curriculum consultant: Debra Voege, M.A.,
science curriculum resource teacher

WEEKLY READER®
PUBLISHING

Please visit our web site at www.garethstevens.com.
For a free color catalog describing our list of high-quality books,
call 1-800-542-2595 (USA) or 1-800-387-3178 (Canada). Our fax: 1-877-542-2596

Library of Congress Cataloging-in-Publication Data

Benduhn, Tea.
    Water power / by Tea Benduhn.
       p. cm. — (Energy for today)
    Includes bibliographical references and index.
    ISBN-10: 0-8368-9264-X — ISBN-13: 978-0-8368-9264-2 (lib. bdg.)
    ISBN-10: 0-8368-9363-8 — ISBN-13: 978-0-8368-9363-2 (softcover)
    1. Water power—Juvenile literature. I. Title.
  TC147.B46 2009
  621.31'2134—dc22
                                      2008012021

This edition first published in 2009 by
Weekly Reader® Books
An Imprint of Gareth Stevens Publishing
1 Reader's Digest Road
Pleasantville, NY 10570-7000 USA

Senior Managing Editor: Lisa M. Herrington
Senior Editor: Brian Fitzgerald
Creative Director: Lisa Donovan
Designer: Ken Crossland
Photo Researcher: Diane Laska-Swanke

Image credits: Cover and title page: © age fotostock/SuperStock; p. 5: © Ace Stock Limited/Alamy; p. 6: © Blend Images/Alamy; p. 7: © Joseph Calev/Shutterstock; p. 9: © Peter Bowater/Alamy; p. 10: © Jan Martin Will/Shutterstock; p. 11 (left): © Stefan Glebowski/Shutterstock; p. 11 (center): © Kameel4u/Shutterstock; p. 11 (right): © Can Balcioglu/Shutterstock; p. 12: © Martin Ruegner/Getty Images; pp. 13, 17: Rob Schuster; p. 15: © Mike Dobel/Alamy; p. 16: Bureau of Reclamation; p. 19: © SueC/Shutterstock; p. 20: © Photofusion Picture Library/Alamy; p. 21: © Picture Partners/Alamy.

Printed in the United States

1 2 3 4 5 6 7 8 9 10 09 08

Table of Contents

Words that appear in the glossary are printed in **boldface** type the first time they occur in the text.

Chapter 1

What Is Water Power?

Have you ever watched a surfer ride a wave? The wave pushes the surfboard forward. Water can also push a boat down a river. Both the surfboard and the boat are moved by water power. Water power is the use of moving water to move an object. Water power is also called hydropower. The Greek word *hydro* means "water."

If you turn on a hose, water flows out the end of it. The water washes dirt off the sidewalk. Turn the nozzle more and the water flow is stronger. What happens if you cover part of the opening at the end of the hose? The water flow is even stronger. It has a lot of power. The stronger the water flow, the more power it has.

Water power pushes a surfboard along an ocean wave.

Water power is a source of **energy**. Energy is the ability to do work. Anything that moves has energy. You have energy! **Kinetic energy** is energy in motion. **Potential energy** is stored. Energy changes from one form to the other. When you sleep, you have potential energy. Your potential energy changes into kinetic energy when you get up and get ready for school.

These children are using energy. Can you find kinetic energy?

Seattle, Washington, gets a lot of its electricity from water power.

Water can have stored and moving energy, too. When water is still, it has potential energy. Water's potential energy changes into kinetic energy when it flows. The energy of flowing water can be used to make electricity. We use electricity to power lights, computers, and televisions.

Chapter 2

Sources of Energy

Today, we get most of our energy from oil, gas, and coal. These energy sources are **fossil fuels**. Fossil fuels formed from the remains of plants and animals that lived millions of years ago. We use fossil fuels to heat our homes, power our cars, and make electricity. Fossil fuels are **nonrenewable resources**. They cannot be replaced. After fossil fuels burn up, they are gone forever.

Most power plants in the United States burn coal to make electricity.

People need fossil fuels, but using them can be harmful. Burning fossil fuels makes **pollution**. Polluted air is dirty and hard to breathe. People and animals can get sick from drinking polluted water. Burning fossil fuels also lets off gases that are causing Earth to slowly heat up. Scientists call this rise in temperature **global warming**.

Global warming may cause ice to melt at the North and South poles. Polar bears and other animals are losing their homes because of the melting ice. The water from melted ice could cause floods in coastal areas.

A polar bear needs ice to survive.

Solid

Gas

Liquid

Water can change from ice to liquid to water vapor and back again.

Water is a great source of energy because it cannot be used up. Water is a **renewable resource**, or a source of energy that can be easily replaced. The amount of water in the world is always the same. Water just changes form. Ice, sleet, and snow are solid water. When ice melts, it turns to liquid water. When water boils or dries up, it turns to a gas called water vapor.

Water changes forms as it moves from air to land and back again. This ongoing change is called the **water cycle**. You've seen the water cycle at work. Water falling from the sky as rain or snow is called **precipitation**. Water may fall into lakes and oceans. It may also flow into rivers or soak into the ground.

We see the water cycle at work during a rain shower.

The Water Cycle

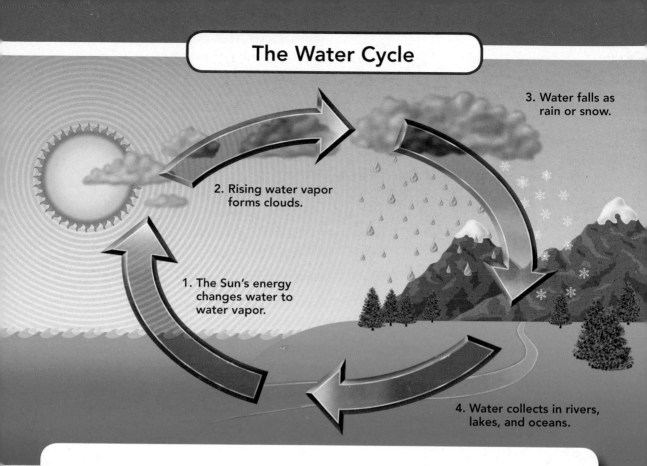

2. Rising water vapor forms clouds.

3. Water falls as rain or snow.

1. The Sun's energy changes water to water vapor.

4. Water collects in rivers, lakes, and oceans.

The Sun heats all the water on Earth's surface. Some water **evaporates**, or changes to water vapor. The vapor rises into the air. High up, the air is cold. Water vapor **condenses**, or changes to a liquid. Water droplets form clouds. As the clouds get heavy, the water falls as rain or snow. The water cycle continues again and again.

Chapter 3

How Water Power Works

People have used water power for thousands of years. In the past, they built waterwheels. A waterwheel has paddles all around its outer edge. The wheel turns as water flows past the paddles. The turning waterwheel can power machines.

To work, a waterwheel needs a steady flow of water. A waterwheel may stop turning when there is no rainfall. A strong water flow, however, could smash a waterwheel. A dam holds back rushing water from a river. Water pools up behind the dam. The stored water can be used for drinking or watering crops. Water can be released from a dam like a waterfall.

The force of flowing water keeps a waterwheel spinning.

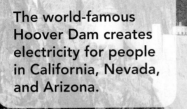

The world-famous Hoover Dam creates electricity for people in California, Nevada, and Arizona.

Running water has a lot of power. The water behind a dam has a lot of potential energy. When that water is released, its energy can be used to make electricity. A hydropower plant is a dam that uses water power to make electricity. Water power is one of the cleanest ways to make energy. A hydropower plant does not make pollution.

A hydropower plant has a gate at the back of the dam. The gate controls the flow of water into a tunnel in the dam. Water released into the tunnel flows past a **turbine**. The turbine is like a huge fan that spins in moving water. The turbine is attached to a **generator**. The generator changes the water's energy into electricity.

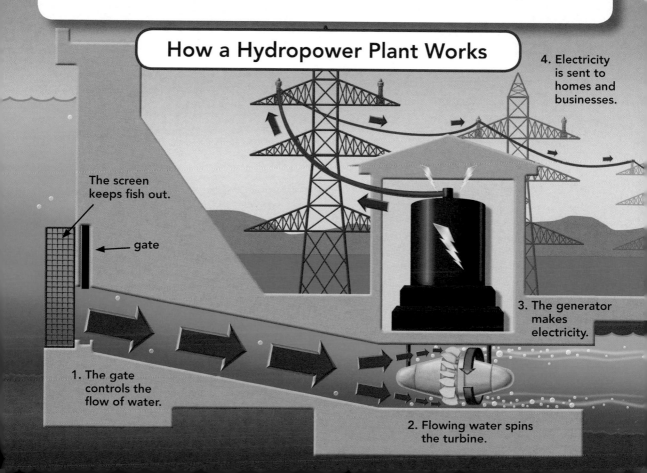

How a Hydropower Plant Works

4. Electricity is sent to homes and businesses.

The screen keeps fish out.

gate

3. The generator makes electricity.

1. The gate controls the flow of water.

2. Flowing water spins the turbine.

Chapter 4

Water Power in the Future

In the United States, we get most of our energy from fossil fuels. Scientists are looking for new ways to use other energy sources. Water power is one of the best renewable resources. It cannot be used up, and it does not make pollution. Today, people in the United States get less than 10 percent of their energy from water power.

Dams block the path of fish that swim in rivers. Many dams have special steps that let fish swim upstream.

Water power is not perfect. Building a dam can flood the land behind it, where the water is held. People and animals can lose their homes from the flood. When the dam holds the water, less water flows out the other side. The changes in water flow can be harmful to people or wildlife in the area. They might not get enough water. People must be careful about where they build water power plants.

Scientists are looking for new ways to turn water into energy. They are looking to oceans, for example. Oceans would be a great source of energy because they hold so much water. Oceans cover more than 70 percent of Earth. Ocean waves are strong. Scientists are working on ways to use wave energy to make electricity.

This hydropower plant is in France. It is the only power plant in the world that makes electricity from ocean waves.

We should try to use less water. You can start by turning off the faucet while you brush your teeth.

In the future, we will need to use many forms of energy. Water power is an important form of energy. Energy from the Sun, wind, and fuels made from plants will also be important. We should try to use less energy, too. We should try to **conserve**, or save, water. For example, remember to turn off the water when you brush your teeth. What are some other ways you can protect Earth's water?

Glossary

condense: to change from water vapor to liquid water

conserve: to save

energy: the ability to do work

evaporate: to change from liquid water to water vapor

fossil fuels: sources of energy, such as oil, gas, and coal, that formed from the remains of plants or animals that lived millions of years ago

generator: a machine that makes electricity or other energy

global warming: the slow rise in Earth's temperature

kinetic energy: energy that is moving

nonrenewable resource: a resource that cannot be used again. Once it is used, it is gone forever. Fossil fuels are nonrenewable resources.

pollution: harmful materials in the environment

potential energy: energy that is stored

precipitation: rain, snow, sleet, or hail

renewable resource: a resource that can be used again. Renewable resources include air, water, sunlight, wind, and plants and animals.

turbine: a machine that turns to create electricity

water cycle: the ongoing movement of water from the land to the air and back again

To Find Out More

Books

Hoover Dam. All Aboard America (series). Julie Murray (Buddy Books, 2005)

How Water Changes. States of Matter (series). Jim Mezzanotte (Weekly Reader Books, 2007)

Water Power. Focus, Energy (series). Meredith Costain (Tandem Library, 2001)

Web Sites

EIA Energy Kid's Page

www.eia.doe.gov/kids/energyfacts/sources/renewable/water.html
Find out more about water power, and learn which states use it the most.

USGS Water Science for Schools

ga.water.usgs.gov/edu/hyhowworks.html
See an animated clip that shows how a hydropower plants makes electricity.

Publisher's note to educators and parents: Our editors have carefully reviewed these web sites to ensure that they are suitable for children. Many web sites change frequently, however, and we cannot guarantee that a site's future contents will continue to meet our high standards of quality and educational value. Be advised that children should be closely supervised whenever they access the Internet.

Index

About the Author

Tea Benduhn writes books and edits a magazine. She lives in the beautiful state of Wisconsin with her husband and two cats. The walls of their home are lined with bookshelves filled with books. Tea says, "I read every day. It is more fun than watching television!"